A BASKETBALL STORY

THE JACKRABBITS VS. THE SEA TURTLES

BY
MILES DAVIS-MAJORS

**ILLUSTRATIONS BY
KAREN B. JONES**

Entrepreneur Press, Publisher
Cover Design: Andrew Welyczko
Production and Composition: Andrew Welyczko
Illustrations: Karen B. Jones

Library of Congress Cataloging-in-Publication Data

Names: Davis-Majors, Miles, author. | Jones, Karen B., illustrator.
Title: A basketball story / by Miles Davis-Majors ; illustrations by Karen
 B. Jones.
Description: Irvine, CA : Entrepreneur Press, 2022. | Audience: Ages 5-7 |
 Audience: Grades K-1 | Summary: "A Basketball Story follow author and
 coach Miles Davis and his youth basketball team, the Jackrabbits, on
 their road to the championship playoffs. This story teaches and
 important moral lesson to stay humble, keep your eyes on the prize, and
 never give up"-- Provided by publisher.
Identifiers: LCCN 2022003436 (print) | LCCN 2022003437 (ebook) | ISBN
 9781642011524 (trade paperback) | ISBN 9781613084649 (epub)
Subjects: LCSH: Basketball--Juvenile literature. | Basketball
 teams--Juvenile literature. | Sportsmanship--Juvenile literature.
Classification: LCC GV885.1 .D38 2022 (print) | LCC GV885.1 (ebook) | DDC
 796.323--dc23/eng/20220325
LC record available at https://lccn.loc.gov/2022003436
LC ebook record available at https://lccn.loc.gov/2022003437

ISBN 978-1-64201-152-4 (paperback) | ISBN 978-1-61308-464-9 (ebook)

Printed in the United States of America

To my 2017 Holmes Elementary School players:

Our basketball season was one of the best times in my life because I always wanted to coach a basketball team coming out of high school.

You guys were the first team I ever coached. You were such characters; no wonder you are in a book! You had this natural chemistry on the court that most elementary schoolers don't have. I feel like it was the reason we won as much as we did. I can still remember you guys doing the fast break, hitting three-pointers, and winning close games. Great memories!

Now we didn't get the outcome we wanted, but we had such a great time throughout the season and especially at SkyZone.

The cool thing is that we can say that we were part of this story. Most importantly, our story will teach young kids to always be humble!

Record 10-0
Holmes Elementary School
Boys and Girls Club of Long Beach

I will remember you guys always and forever.

Coach Miles

The school bell rang at Davis Elementary School, and the students were out. Some students began walking home. Some students waited for their parents. And some students headed to the after-school program, **The Girls & Boys Academy.** This is where our story begins.

It was a special time for the kids at The Girls & Boys Academy. It was early spring, which meant it was time for the annual elementary school basketball season. The team at The Girls & Boys Academy was called the Jackrabbits. The kids couldn't wait to sign up!

Ms. Carol, the director of The Girls & Boys Academy, greeted the kids with exciting news. "Basketball season is coming up," she said with a smile, "and this year we have a new coach! His name is Coach Miles. Raise your hand if you want to try out for the basketball team!" The kids raised their hands and cheered.

They'd lost in the playoffs the year before. This year, they wanted to win the championship!

BASKETBALL TRYOUTS

The kids hurried to the gym to meet their new coach. Coach Miles was in the basketball gym, waiting to meet them. "Hi kids," he said. "I'm so glad to be here. You know, I used to coach the Sea Turtles at Barton Elementary. They're pretty good, but I think you Jackrabbits can be better. What do you say?" The kids cheered excitedly, ready to get to work.

Coach Miles and the Jackrabbits started practicing for their first game right away. They ran drills, practiced their fundamentals, and they learned how to work together. The Jackrabbits were ready!

The Jackrabbit's first game was against the Sea Turtles. The Sea Turtles had done well last season but they had lost in the playoffs too. Many of their best players hadn't graduated yet, so this year they were likely to be one of the top teams in the league.

In their very first game, the Jackrabbits played so well together. They moved fast, played smart, and had fun doing it. When the clock hit zero, the Jackrabbits had beaten the Sea Turtles by three points!

As the Jackrabbits took their first-ever team picture, Coach Miles knew he had a good team. A team that could win a lot of games. Maybe even the championship! But he had to find a way to motivate them.

Coach Miles thought long and hard. Finally, he came up with an idea. The next day before practice, Coach Miles said, "You guys did great, but I know you can do even better. So, I'm making you a promise. If we make it through the season undefeated, 10-0. I'll take the whole team to the trampoline park FUNZone!" The kids cheered, determined to win their prize!

Coach Miles's plan worked! The Jackrabbits trained hard. They played hard. And they won a lot!

Over at Barton Elementary, the Sea Turtles learned about the Jackrabbit's 10-0 reward. "I heard that if the Jackrabbits go 10-0 this season, they get to go to FUNZone!" said one of the players. "Let's not let that happen! We can beat them. We just have to believe in ourselves."

The Sea Turtles had already lost to the Jackrabbits once, which put them in second place in the mid-season standings. They would have one more game against the Jackrabbits at the end of the season. The Sea Turtles wanted to win. They wanted to prevent the Jackrabbits from having an undefeated season and getting to go to FUNZone. They knew that if they believed in themselves, they could do it!

Mid-Season League Standings

Jackrabbits 7-0
Sea Turtles 6-1
Eagles 4-3
Bears 2-5

Game after game, the Jackrabbits kept winning. Their undefeated record went up and up … 7-0, 8-0, 9-0. They'd won so many games that now they felt like they couldn't lose. Coach Miles was proud of his team, but he was also worried. Coach Miles realized that his kids had become cocky. At practice, they stopped working as hard as they had at the beginning of the season. Coach Miles knew that their overconfidence could ruin their chances for a 10-0 record.

Finally, it was time for the last game of the season—the number one team, the Jackrabbits vs the number two team, the Sea Turtles. If the Jackrabbits won, they would finish the season undefeated and get to go to FUNZone. But the Sea Turtles were ready, too. They wanted to beat the number one team.

It was a tough game. Parents cheered as the score went back and forth. Both teams put in all they had, but in the end when the buzzer sounded, the Jackrabbits won by two points. They had done it! They had gone undefeated the whole season.

The Sea Turtles were upset that they lost. Some of them cried because they wanted to win so badly. After losing twice to the Jackrabbits in one season, the Sea Turtles were left with one more opportunity for a possible rematch—in the playoffs.

21

Coach Miles was proud of his team, but he was still worried. With only days to go before the playoffs, he decided to have a game plan meeting with his team. He wanted the team to know what their strategies were going to be before the playoffs started. But the kids wouldn't listen to Coach Miles. They were so sure they would win that they just joked around and didn't pay attention to the strategies that Coach Miles wanted them to do.

A few days later, Coach Miles had to substitute teach at the Sea Turtles' school. Looking out his classroom window, he saw the Sea Turtles practicing hard for the playoffs. Coach Miles's fear was coming true. His team was so sure they'd win because they went 10-0 that they stopped practicing as hard as they should have. Coach Miles could tell that the Sea Turtles wanted to beat the Jackrabbits. They were so focused. They wanted to beat the Jackrabbits just as much as they wanted to win the championship.

It was time for the playoffs. The Jackrabbits were the number one seed, and they won their first playoff game to lead them to the championship game. The second seed, the Sea Turtles, won their game too. The Jackrabbits and the Sea Turtles would meet again for the third time to play for the championship.

Before the championship game began, Coach Miles went to the locker room to check on his team to see if they were ready. But when he got there, he found the kids were even more sure of themselves. They weren't even thinking about the championship game against the Sea Turtles! Some of them were sleeping on the floor. Coach Miles knew this wasn't a good sign.

The third showdown began. The Sea Turtles had already lost twice, and they were determined not to lose again.

As Coach Miles expected The Jackrabbits didn't come to play their best.

The Jackrabbits didn't even play defense. Instead, they were having a conversation in the middle of the game. Coach Miles was embarrassed for his team.

The Jackrabbit's overconfidence had made them believe that they were going to win just because they showed up to the game. As Coach Miles watched the game, his fear became true. The Sea Turtles kept their focus and won by one point. They beat the Jackrabbits' undefeated streak and became The Girls & Boys Academy's elementary school division basketball champions! The once undefeated Jackrabbits were left sad and crying.

As Coach Miles watched his kids cry, he knew that he had to teach them a lesson. He went into the locker room and said, "They won because we played with too much overconfidence and we were lazy. And they played hard and tried their best. Just because we were 10-0, and we beat them twice before, doesn't mean you shouldn't have tried your best. We have to learn from this. Okay... now let's go back to the court, shake their hands, and tell them 'Good Game!'"

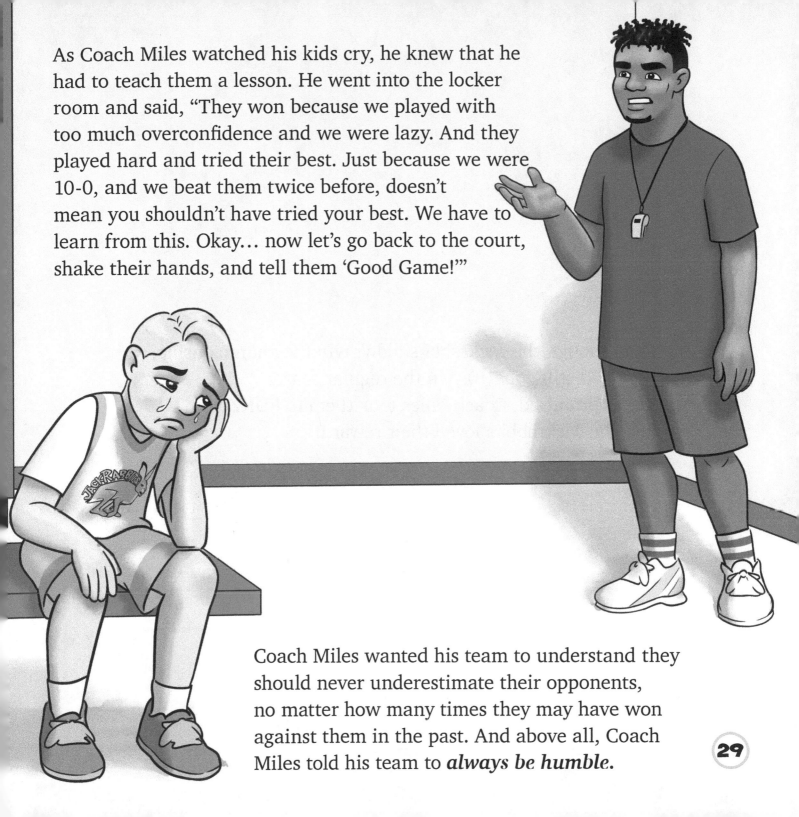

Coach Miles wanted his team to understand they should never underestimate their opponents, no matter how many times they may have won against them in the past. And above all, Coach Miles told his team to **always be humble.**

Even though the Jackrabbits didn't win the championship,
they had still gone 10-0 in the regular season.
So, as promised, Coach Miles took them to FUNZone,
and the Jackrabbits loved their reward!

CPSIA information can be obtained
at www.ICGtesting.com
Printed in the USA
JSHW030139100422
24773JS00007B/8